YOUR KNOWLEDGE HAS VALUE

- We will publish your bachelor's and master's thesis, essays and papers

- Your own eBook and book - sold worldwide in all relevant shops

- Earn money with each sale

Upload your text at www.GRIN.com and publish for free

Ulrike Ditzel

Cultural Differences in Business Life - Understanding German and American Business Culture

GRIN Verlag

Bibliografische Information der Deutschen Nationalbibliothek:

Die Deutsche Bibliothek verzeichnet diese Publikation in der Deutschen Nationalbibliografie; detaillierte bibliografische Daten sind im Internet über http://dnb.d-nb.de/ abrufbar.

Dieses Werk sowie alle darin enthaltenen einzelnen Beiträge und Abbildungen sind urheberrechtlich geschützt. Jede Verwertung, die nicht ausdrücklich vom Urheberrechtsschutz zugelassen ist, bedarf der vorherigen Zustimmung des Verlages. Das gilt insbesondere für Vervielfältigungen, Bearbeitungen, Übersetzungen, Mikroverfilmungen, Auswertungen durch Datenbanken und für die Einspeicherung und Verarbeitung in elektronische Systeme. Alle Rechte, auch die des auszugsweisen Nachdrucks, der fotomechanischen Wiedergabe (einschließlich Mikrokopie) sowie der Auswertung durch Datenbanken oder ähnliche Einrichtungen, vorbehalten.

Imprint:

Copyright © 2006 GRIN Verlag GmbH
Druck und Bindung: Books on Demand GmbH, Norderstedt Germany
ISBN: 978-3-638-81039-5

This book at GRIN:

http://www.grin.com/en/e-book/62926/cultural-differences-in-business-life-understanding-german-and-american

GRIN - Your knowledge has value

Der GRIN Verlag publiziert seit 1998 wissenschaftliche Arbeiten von Studenten, Hochschullehrern und anderen Akademikern als eBook und gedrucktes Buch. Die Verlagswebsite www.grin.com ist die ideale Plattform zur Veröffentlichung von Hausarbeiten, Abschlussarbeiten, wissenschaftlichen Aufsätzen, Dissertationen und Fachbüchern.

Visit us on the internet:

http://www.grin.com/

http://www.facebook.com/grincom

http://www.twitter.com/grin_com

Faculty of Philosophy
Intercultural Business Communication
- Interculture USA/Germany -James McDonald

Theme:

- Cultural Differences in Business Life -
Understanding German and American Business culture

BWL

date: 31.01.2006

Table of Contents

TABLE OF CONTENTS II
LIST OF FIGURES III
1. INTRODUCTION 1
2. NECESSITY OF INTERCULTURAL UNDERSTANDINGS 2
   2.1 WHAT IS CULTURE? 3
   2.2 THEORETICAL CONSTRUCTS OF CULTURE 4
      2.2.1 Hofstedes Dimensions of Culture 4
      2.2.2 Halls Model of Cultures 6
3. DIFFERENCES IN AMERICAN AND GERMAN BUSINESS CULTURES 7
   3.1 DIFFERENT WAYS OF SAYING 8
   3.2 HOFSTEDES MOST SIGNIFICANT DIFFERENCES 12
      3.2.1 Individuality versus Collectivism 12
      3.2.2 Uncertainty Avoidance 13
      3.2.3 Motivation 14
   3.3 FURTHER DIFFERENCES 15
4. CONCLUDING REMARKS 16
BIBLIOGRAPHY 18

List of Figures

- **Figure 1:** According to Hofstede, G. (1991), "Cultures and Organizations", McGraw-Hill, London.

1. Introduction

Globalization has led to remarkable changes in the way we conduct the world's business. International Mergers and acquisitions are en vogue today. The advantages quoted by managers include advantages of scale, increased shareholder value, access to new markets, lower overheads and so on. The number of international mergers and acquisitions between German and American companies increased a lot during the last years, as well.

At the beginning there are high hopes and elation connected with the deal. But the long-term reality, however, is much the opposite. At least 50 percent of all international mergers and acquisition activity fails, no matter how the success is measured.[1]

There are also lots of companies who failed, who are therefore not able to benefit from some positive synergy effects like cost reductions. Why did that happen?

A survey tried to analyze the reasons for this. The surprising result was that just 30% of the failures were attributed to the "hard factors" of business, like planning, finance or technology. For the rest, the reason lay in the so-called "soft factors", which contain cultural and organizational behaviour.[2]

Somewhat less acknowledged, although hardly disputed, is the positive and negative impact of cultural aspects on the success of M&A activity.[3]

The following work reveals the differences between American and German business culture and also analyzes its historical and social background. Thereby, the main goal is to disprove that American and German business styles are almost similar.

Furthermore, at the end the reader should know more about the existing differences between the two nations, because their unawareness leads to the failures of M&A.

In the second chapter there is theoretical basis information which helps to reach a better understanding of this work. Thereafter comes the main part about the existing differences between Germans and Americans. Because there are plenty of them, it is just possible to take a brief view on a certain field of life. For this reason the author picks a few, those which seem to be the most relevant differences between the German and American business world.

---

[1] Forstmann, St. (1998), p. 57.
[2] Schmidt P., (2002b)
[3] Forstmann, St. (1998), p. 57.

In every part, the author is going to illustrate the differences by means of examples[4]. The main question which is answered in this work is: *WHY* do these different characteristics exist? Where do they come from?

2. Necessity of Intercultural Understandings

As the reader has seen in the introduction part, the main reason for the failure of M&A laid in the "soft-factors" containing cultural and organizational behaviour.

The main problem of many persons in leading positions is the fact that they are not aware of the existing cultural differences, or just underestimate them. And this is a major problem between Americans and Germans. Executives in both countries say that their cultures are almost the same.

On the one hand this seems to be true. Both countries have a strong Anglo – Saxon background, which means they are quite pragmatic in the way they do business. In addition, Germans and Americans have a propensity to concentrate on one activity at a time. Both value punctuality, are results-oriented, as well as competitive and practical.[5] Another fact which causes this opinion is that many Germans speak English very well, if not even excellent. The common western mindset of these two cultures intensifies that they appear to be similar.[6]

As a result both sides expect each other to think, communicate and behave the same.

People, who share this opinion, tend to become a victim of the most common mistake in U.S. – German business relations – the "trap of similarity",[7] the synonym for the fact, that the German and American culture looks very similar at the surface.

But beneath there are existing differences. And because they are not expected, their effect can be even more damaging for every business relation between a German and an American company.

The most important thing to do is to make you aware of the cultural differences – or more general – aware of the differences in the "soft factors", including also the organizational differences.

---

[4] Which we will see, is also a typical German attribute.
[5] www.agcc.de
[6] www.german-connection.com
[7] www.amcham.com

But to be able to do this you need to know about the existing differences and even more important you need to get an understanding about your own culture and the culture you are dealing with. Therefore it is necessary to analyze "What is culture?" and afterwards describe the differences.

2.1 What is Culture?

The word culture can have a number of meanings. As a basic for this work culture is seen as a system of shared beliefs, values, customs, behaviors, ideas and artifacts that members of society use to cope with their world and with another. All these are transmitted from generation to generation through learning.[8]

Culture is all what people as members of a society have, think and do. Everybody is part of a specific culture, through the process which is known as socialization. This process of socialization is nothing we are aware of. Culture is so much a part of ourselves that we are hardly able to figure it out or express it. For human beings it is not imaginable to live another way of life than the own one.[9]

Quite often we are not even aware of our own culture just until the moment we were confronted with another culture. This instant in which two different culture patterns clash together leads automatically to confusion and disagreements.

A perfectly metaphor for the terminus "culture" is the construct of an "iceberg". Only a few aspects are evident – just like the top of the iceberg. These are the identifiable elements for example language, clothing or customs. On the other hand there is the part of the iceberg which we do not see. This is where the more important elements come from, the ones which lead to a deeper meaning and understanding of a culture. These values guide the thoughts and actions of people.[10]

---

[8] www.umanitoba.ca
[9] Schmidt, P. (2002), p. 14.
[10] Bolten Skript „Einführung IWK"

2.2 Theoretical Constructs of Culture

The most interesting question of all is why do people act the way they do? Where do these differences come from? What is the reason for the behaviour of the members of the country? Scientists developed models to explain why people in different countries do the same things differently. Of course, these models can not be complete, because they base on percentiles and they are not supposed to be absolutely correct or the best ones. But they should be seen as a help, as a practical method to "read" and understand a culture.

The two models of *Geert Hofstede* and *Edward Hall* are useful to characterize typical behaviours of people. This allows a comparison between two people, which is the supposed to be part of this work. For this reason the two concepts are explained in the following passages.

2.2.1 Hofstedes Dimensions of Culture

In 1980 Geert Hofstede made a fascinating study related to the fundamental values and behaviours in working life. He collected data in IBM subsidiaries in 66 countries and analyzed their habits. Because the employers came from one enterprise, one can classify the differences to the national cultures. He developed a model which identified four primary dimensions to explain work related differences in behaviour:

- Individualism vs. Collectivism
- Power Distance
- Uncertainty Avoidance
- Masculinity vs. Femininity[11]

---

[11] Hofstede, G. (1991), p. 13ff.

Figure 1: Hofstedes Results

Land	Individualism	Power Distance	Uncertainty Avoidance	Masculinity
Germany	67	35	65	66
USA	91	40	46	62

0= low; 100= high

In reference to the figures in: Hofstede, G. (1991).

Individualism vs. Collectivism

In individualistic cultures people tend to take care of their selves and their families rather than of others. They value freedom and personal time. Every single person is appreciated. The emphasis is put on socio – economic goals rather than on goals for the group.

In contrary, in collectivistic cultures people are integrated into a strong, cohesive group that provides protection. The members of this culture subordinate their individual necessaries under the fortune of the group.[12]

Power Distance

The second dimension is the power distance, which shows to what degree a culture accepts the unequal power distribution within a culture.

A society with a minimal power distance refuses social classes and hierarchical structures. On the other side there are the cultures with high power distance, where different classes are accepted. The position of the individual in the society influences the way this person acts and also the way others treat this person.[13]

Uncertainty Avoidance

The dimension of uncertainty avoidance expresses to what degree a culture feels endangered in unpredictable and unclear situations and therefore tries to avoid those situations through the establishment of rules, the intolerance towards unmoral ideas and behaviours.

This means that in a land with a high degree of uncertainty avoidance there are much more rules of conduct, written and unwritten ones. As a result the laws are stricter; they put much more emphasis on fulfilling tasks correctly.

---

[12] Hofstede, G. (1991), p. 49ff.
[13] Hofstede, G. (1991), p. 27ff.

Cultures which accept more uncertainty tend to be more relaxed in unknown situations. This also includes a higher willingness to take risks.[14]

Femininity vs. Masculinity

For Hofstede a masculine society is ruled by hard values such as money, success, self assertion, and competition. Men and women have fixed roles, which are orientated on the traditional assignments of roles.

A feminine culture puts more emphasis on soft values such as relations, caring about each other, quality of life or service. The roles of men and women are less strictly separated and often equal.[15]

2.2.2 Halls Model of Cultures

The American scientist Hall used the expression "communication" to find a way to understand cultures. He defines culture as a system which is ready to create, send, save and work on information. Communication is the common string which goes through all cultures. He says that the way how people communicate is depending on the context. This again is the information which goes together with an occasion.[16]

Communication is the process of conveying i.e. information or feelings. It means the encoding and sending of a message by using the right representation a well as a correct decoding of these representations upon reception.[17]

Cultures with communication depending on context and not depending on it

Hall classifies cultures on a scale from "high-" to "low-context". The first ones are depending on context, which means that communication is implicit. The notification is not just transmitted trough words but also through body language, the circumstances and the relation between the involved people.

People in cultures with communication not depending on context, put the emphasis on the acoustic content in a conversation not on the context. Therefore communication is explicit.

---

[14] Hofstede, G. (1991), p. 109ff.
[15] Hofstede, G. (1991), p. 79ff.
[16] Schmidt, P. (2002a), p. 19.
[17] Schmidt, P. (2004).

Words do not need the comprehension of the culture to be translated, they are clear and direct. In this kind of culture there is a separation between personal relations, work and other aspects of the daily life. Americans and Germans are both "low-context cultures".[18]

Societies with fixed and flexible time planning
Another important aspect of culture is time. Hall declares that there are two different ways dealing with time which are important for international economy.

Firstly there is the society with a fixed time planning or also called "monochronic society". There, people are focused on a specific time to just one activity. Time planning is very important and members of this society speak about time as if it would be a real object. The expression "Time is money" is a good example for it. Germany and the U.S.A. belong to this category.[19]

In opposition of what has been stated is the "polychronic" system. This one is characterized by the fact that many activities can occur simultaneously and that is there much more emphasis on human beings and relations. The present activity is more important than former plans or schedules.[20]

3. Differences in American and German Business Cultures

With the given theoretical information from the preceding paragraph it should be now much easier to understand the following representations.

To write about all facts concerning differences between German and American business cultures would end up in a book and is therefore much too detailed. For this reason the author is going to concentrate on the major existing differences in business life. Every section includes real examples to support this theme in a certain way. Thereafter follows the explanation of the differences including the deeper roots of them.

---

[18] Hofstede, G. (1991), p. 60.
[19] Schmidt, P. (2002a), p. 19f.
[20] Schmidt, P. (2002a), p. 19f.

3.1 Different Ways of Saying

As it was shown in the former chapter, communication in general means the encoding and sending of a message by using the right representation.[21] This can be verbal, written, nonverbal or musical. All of the possible forms of representations contain unspoken rules which can create subtle and even meaningful misunderstandings, if not understood. Therefore, the danger of any encoding occurs when one comes from another culture with different values and rules. The fact, that a message depends on the perception of the receiver and not what the presenter thinks has been expressed, intensifies this problem.[22]

German business conversation emphasizes content and downplays emotions and personal relationships. They value honesty and directness and they love examples. Also Germans estimate detailed explanations which often lead to the fact that they give many details.
In addition Germans explore all sides of an issue, even if this means being unpleasant, confrontational and spending lots of time analyzing a problem.[23] The main goal of German conversation is to get to the truth (Wahrheitssuche). This explains why Germans usually put this strong emphasis on content and keep the personal separate. Closely related to this is a strong emphasis on being objective and credible. Their value for frankness affects language usage. It makes their conversations fact-oriented and formal. Generally, Germans are very direct when it comes to offering criticism and giving orders. Even confrontations with superiors are not unusual.[24]
An adequate example would be the 8 o'clock news on ARD. The announcer is the quintessence of German objectivity, speaking with his steady monotonic voice and absolutely showing no emotions, no matter what's happening in the world.
In German business settings, if someone wants to put more emphasis on the personal beyond the professional, it can actually be considered instructive. People fell uncomfortable.[25] Another common German verbal habit is the frequent use of the modal verbs "müssen" and "sollen". The often usage of these words make their style stronger and less diplomatic, as e.g. the American.[26]

---
[21] Compare Chapter 2.2
[22] Schmidt, P. (2004).
[23] Schmidt, P. (2002a) p. 90f.
[24] Schmidt, P. (2002b).
[25] Schmidt, P. (2003b)
[26] Schmidt, P. (2002b).

But why are Germans so "objective-minded"? A lot of research has been done on this topic and the results brought up historical reasons for this.

The first one is the influence of the Lutheranism. One major point according to Luther was to keep the emotional separated from the sacred. In his opinion such feelings were not necessary part of faith. As time passes, two strong values became secularized in Germany. Not just the superiority of objective reasoning but also the idea that you prove your love to God through the diligent mastery of a craft. One's love to God was expressed by performing tasks and objectively as one could. Germans see this as a calling in life (Berufung). The phrase: "I have to do my duty" expresses this value. The socialist Max Weber called this the "Protestant work ethic".[27]

A really strong emphasis on the German culture and with this on the German way of communication has the fact that Germany suffered under a high number of wars. It begun with the Thirty Year War where over 35% of its population was lost. Other tragic conflicts like the Napoleonic War, the Austro-Prussian War and then the two World Wars followed. In the last one, the Holocausts brought disgrace and shame upon the German people. Not only death and mass destruction but also massive financial losses were the results of these wars.

According to this tragic and violent past it is not surprising that these wars and their consequences have played a major role in the German society and therefore in the development of the culture.[28]

On the other hand there are the Americans. They describe German conversations as too serious, with too many facts and figures. Although their way of communication is according to Hall's division a "low-context" - the same as the Germans - there are major differences in the communication style. The main one is that Americans accentuate both: the content as well as the personal. Most Americans prefer to break the ice quickly and operate in an informal manner. The focus of communication is usually on positive feedback and briefness, quickly leading to action. Americans have a completely different conception of directness. Because they value being liked, they are more direct than Germans when it comes to expressing pleasure or revealing personal details to people they do not know well or giving praise and compliments.[29] In general it can be described as the American openness.

---

[27] Schmidt, P. (2003b).
[28] Schmidt, P. (2003b).
[29] Schmidt, P. (2002a) p. 88f.

But why are Americans so open?

The reasons for the American openness, also known as "friendliness" are mainly found in the historical development of the country.[30]

The USA was founded by northern European settlers, mostly from Great Britain, who were fleeing because of religious persecution in their own country. These people were forced to start a new life elsewhere. They had no use for the traditions of the societies which had rejected them but they where eager for new ideas.

One of these thoughts came from the French philosopher Jean-Jacques Rousseau and his belief in the goodness of nature. His idea contained that it was in man's nature to be good meant that a man could improve his condition in life. Rousseau had the opinion that this includes an economic benefit. A society would be highly efficient and dynamic when the man believes in the goodness of others. This mutual trust will eliminate the time-consuming process of doubting and judging. When building a nation, decisions have to be made quickly. "Yes or no" and "time is money" become the norm. And that's exactly the situation in which the early immigrants had been at this time. It is a very simplistic notion of life which ignored the complexities and nuances that our existence continually presents. But this was what America needed to develop itself and what turned out to be incredibly successful for both immigrants and their American offspring. [31]

As a result of the acceptance of these thoughts and in combination with rich natural resources developed another behavioural trait which won't be found elsewhere in the world: the "pursuit of happiness".[32] When the immigrants arrived at the "New World" they had plenty of opportunities which they could take to fulfil their own "happiness". Everybody was able to move up the social ladder. If they had new ideas and visions, they would even more succeed.

This upward mobility relies on positive reinforcement which is still today deeply rooted in the American social interaction and communication. It reveals in the habit that Americans tend to give much more compliments. A short "Well done!" is to be sure. If they have to give negative feedback then this is in a reserved way. Personal critics are absolutely disdained.[33]

---

[30] Schmidt, P. (2003a).
[31] Schmidt, P. (2002).
[32] Schmidt, P. (2003b).
[33] Schmidt, P. (2004).

Even in 1831 this behaviour was already noted. Alexis de Tocqueville said in his book "Democracy in America" about them:

> *"In dealing with strangers, Americans seem to be impatient with the slightest criticism and insatiable for praise."*

Another reason for the openness to all strangers has to do with the immigrants as well. There were an increasing number of immigrants who came to the USA – beginning massively with the Irish during the Great Famine of 1845-1849. The new immigrants needed help getting started in America and so they just had to learn very quickly to reach out to people they didn't know. They didn't have the luxury of keeping other people at a certain distance.

In the later half of the 1800s when the early Americans started to move toward the Pacific coast, they didn't worry about privacy. On the contrary, the problem these people had was how they can find fellowship in this wide-open and unknown land. To survive during these hard and long journeys, it was necessary to be within a bigger group. Dangers could occur everywhere but being in a group increased the chance to survive and consequently reach the aim they wanted. Friends and allies were necessary to conquer nature and build the country. Once again being open was the only possible way of acting.[34]

The shown facts do explain a lot more than just the different ways of communication. Actually, the historical background is the reason for most of the characteristics of Germans and Americans. And as a consequence, because they were very dissimilar they leaded to a different character.

Example

An adequate example for the clash of styles can be found when Daimler and Chrysler started their merger in 1998. For their first joint board meeting they decided that every company would present itself. Of course everybody wanted to make a good impression to their counterpart. However, both sides had completely different ideas about what made up a good presentation.

The Germans began with a long introduction, the history of the company, model range and other parts packed with details and details. The presenter spoke over two hours, rigid and with a monotonic voice. The Americans, on the other hand, got straight to the point, basically demonstrating their model range. They used lots of showy effects and easy to remember statements. The presenter was enthusiastic about what he said, which had been

---

[34] Schmidt, P. (2003b).

reflected in his body language. At the end, both sides thought they did a good job. But as it was mentioned earlier in this work, in communication the audience determines the message, not the speaker. And therefore one might read in newspapers quite different perceptions about the encounter. The Germans found the American behaviour absolutely superficial coupled with "optimism gone overboard." Whereas for Americans the German presentation was "an absolute information overkill". [35]

3.2 Hofstedes most significant differences

To continue the analysis why Germans and Americans have different cultural patterns, one can use Hofstedes model which helps to characterize and explain differential conducts. According to the data, the Dutch social scientist has collected; there are two dimensions which demonstrate how differently Americans and Germans see their working worlds or better how differently they act in business life.

"Individuality vs. Collectivism" and "uncertainty avoidance" are the sections with the highest measured gap between both nations.

3.2.1 Individuality versus Collectivism

As a result of Hofstedes survey, the United States show the highest values for individualism among all 50 countries asked. The individualistic attitude of Americans is mainly expressed in their need to responsibility, independence and self fulfilment.[36] People in these countries and so is the U.S.A., are mostly concerned about themselves and their families. Progress is seen as the result of individual effort. Mobility is the rule, in all terms, where one works and where one lives.

Germans tend to be less individualistic. They see themselves as part of a group and therefore subordinating individual needs to the common good. Opinions are often determined by the group and ideas like solidarity and harmony are important. Germans put much more emphasis on relationships.[37] They take friendships very serious and would not call somebody their friend if they are not close to each other.

---

[35] Schmidt, P. (2002b)
[36] Hofstede, G. (1991), p. 171.
[37] Schmidt, P. (2004).

This is a major difference of both countries. A real friendship includes responsibility and duty, and these values are the opposite of the American believe in freedom and independence. [38]

3.2.2 Uncertainty Avoidance

Adapting to change and coping with uncertainty is the second major area where Americans and Germans have a different level.

Germans tend to keep risks to an absolute minimum. Everything has to be ordered and structured. The more structure something has, the better. Almost nothing is improvised.

A high number of rules, laws and prohibitions – written as well as unwritten - reflect the German need to avoid every kind of uncertainty.[39] To keep this kind of order, they strictly separate private life from working life. Friendships tend to have the same effect. A real friendship is equivalent to a protection against the insecure world.[40] The need for order in the society is as well reflected in business life. So are existing strict roles for every employee. A description of the position includes an exact definition of the field of responsibility. Germans feel secure, when they have an exactly defined place in the social order. The phenomenon to have a job over a long period of time, which is absolutely common in Germany, is as well a consequence of avoiding uncertainty. To have a job which they can do over years is similar to a certain level of security.[41]

But there is also a positive side of this behaviour. Germans are rational, disciplined and hard working. They are brilliant in organizing and planning. In business life this is a good attribute. All in all Germans need a long time for planning before starting a project, but failures are much more reduced through this way.

Americans in comparison have a much lower level of uncertainty avoidance. In business life that means they take risks and try new things. Also changing jobs quite frequently is absolutely normal in the U.S.A. Americans instinctively share more of their personality on the job. They do not separate both areas as the Germans do. In fact, Americans do not act that differently at work than they do when they are out with friends.

---

[38] Schmidt, P. (2002a) p. 42f.
[39] Schmidt, P. (2002a) p. 27f.
[40] Schmidt, P. (2002a) p. 42.
[41] Schmidt, P. (2002a) p. 60ff.

Example

When it comes to the point in business relations when team work needs to be done, these differences in working culture can lead to massive problems.

In 1995, psychologist Silvia Schroll-Machl examined the reasons American-German projects often failed. It became clear that at the point where problems occurred, differences in problem-solving led to misunderstandings and confusions. [42]

Because of the German tendency to avoid uncertainty they need much more detailed information and discussion at the outset of a project. They considered all of the possible difficulties and plan hypothetical solutions. Germans wanted to make sure that everything would be done correctly and every element possible kept under control. It was essential to find a consensus. The action-oriented Americans found these discussions boring and a waste of time. They want to get down to work. They do not think about all problems which might arise, because they don not have this deeply implemented "need to avoid uncertainty". During her research Schroll-Machl examined even more points which evoked problems between both sides and therefore generated a negative atmosphere in the whole team.[43] The study makes clear that if these differences are dealt with at the beginning, the chances for the success of intercultural groups or projects increase enormously.

3.2.3 Motivation

To understand motivation within a culture one has to look at the social values and assumptions. As it was already said at the beginning of this work, Hofstede estimated the amount of masculinity and femininity in a society. With these figures one is able to see how guerdon and fulfilling essentials of life influences the motivation. He discovered that in a masculine culture, money, title and other material guerdons support motivating a person. Whereas in a feminine culture, better social welfare benefits or free time are the relevant aspects for motivation.

The U.S. is considered to be a masculine society with a pro-active and optimistic approach to life. They see themselves as ambitious, hardworking, innovative and energetic. Success depends only on how much you want it. There is a minimum amount of team spirit, but most of the time they try to work by themselves, because everybody is responsible for his own destiny.

---

[42] Schmidt, P. (2004).
[43] Schmidt, P. (2004).

All these factors lead to a hard competition, which, on the one hand brings economical growth but on the other hand left no space for losers. Their own career is obviously more important than the goals of the company they work for.

Germany also has a masculine society, but with feminine undertones. Like Americans they are ambitious and competitive. But at the same time they prefer to work collectively and following a plan, again also because of their wish to avoid uncertainty. Government, industry and unions collaborate to establish a politic of mutual benefits, a system also called the social-market economy. The end result is consensus and a sense of public welfare. Like in America salary is important, but similar important are quality of life and working relations. Germans are more loyal to the company they work for than Americans. But this again means that workers expect more benefits such as six weeks vacations

These different values affect employee motivation as well as compensation and are reflected in the different salary structure.[44]

Example

A really perfect example is DaimlerChrysler. Their biggest problem after their merger was harmonizing pay structures. A German worker earned 20.000$ more a year than his American colleague. But these costs can be considered as a long term strategy, related to the cultural differences. It helps to keep up a high level of morality, creates loyalty and a sense of duty within the workers.[45] Schrempp, the former head of Daimler, said that the strict rules and the security[46] the German workers have, would avoid strikes and leads to the fact that the employees would have a deeply identification with their company and as a result take this as a motivation and work efficiently.[47]

Whereas Chrysler workers have less holidays, work more hours per week than their German colleagues and do have the security because they do not have this social system which we have in Germany.

3.3 Further Differences

As you can see there are a number of differences between Americans and Germans in business world. But these are not all. Therefore this chapter gives a brief overview over a few more.

---

[44] Schmidt, P. (2002a) p. 71.
[45] Schmidt, P. (2002a) p. 71.
[46] Because of the existing welfare system, agreements with trade unions and so on.
[47] Appel, H.; Hein, C. (1998), p. 255f.

So take for example, the word "manager". It is used in both languages – but the actual expectation of the way this person has to act in a company is extremely different.

The Americans think that a manager has to motivate the workers, controlling the quality and make sure that the job is done properly.

Whereas in Germany, one expects that a manager just gives the tasks and then pulls himself out of this. The workers are trained to solve problems by themselves and they see this way of working like a challenge – they can show their skills.

The tendency to perfectionism is another reason why managers in Germany do not see any reason to motivate their staff. They assume that the workers do the best they can in their job.[48]

Not being aware of these cultural differences – even though this example is just the interpretation of one single word – can lead to fatal consequences.

VW[49] and WalMart – both well known and successful companies – had to experience this themselves.[50] They tried to establish companies in for them foreign countries with simply overtaking their own way of managing.[51] The result for both was an immense loss of money.[52]

4. Concluding Remarks

Quite often culture is perceived by the direct comparison of two different cultures. But only knowing the dissimilarity is not enough for the individuals, because they do not get the access to the other cultures. More important is the conscious interaction with the other cultural partner. This is what intercultural learning is about. It just means the examination with the strange and the willingness to change oneself. Does anybody has the knowledge about the existing differences then he will harmonize his behaviour with the exceptions of his counterpart and misperceptions and misunderstandings will be avoided.

In an increasingly globalized world market companies need to acquire these effective intercultural competencies in order to avoid miscommunication, prevent misunderstandings and avert mistakes and to gain any kind of success.

---

[48] Schmidt, P. (2001).
[49] VW set up a factory for the "Rabbit" in Pennsylvania in the early 80s.
[50] Knorr, A. (2003).
[51] WalMart (American company) settled in the German food – store – market.
[52] www.agcc.de

One should always try to analyze cultural differences and ask oneself "Why do they act the way they do?" If we do that, the gap between the two dynamic countries Germany and the U.S. will be closer together. Negative, counterproductive stereotypes and misperceptions are bound to happen, if we do not consciously understand different styles. But not just in business situations – every time two individuals with different cultural and social background communicate with each other, they should keep in mind that there are differences. And maybe they should talk about it, make their perspectives clear – practice "meta communication".

Bibliography

1. Appel, H.; Hein, C. (1998), „Der DaimlerChrysler Deal", 2.Auflage, Deutsche Verlags-Anstalt, Stuttgart.
2. Forstmann, St. (1998), "Managing cultural differences in Cross-cultural Mergers and Acquisitions", in Gertsen, M. (1998), "Cultural Dimensions of International Mergers and Acquisitions", Berlin.
3. Hofstede, G. (1991), "Cultures and Organizations", McGraw-Hill, London.
4. Knorr, A.; Arndt, A. (2003), "Why did Wal-Mart fail in Germany?" in Knorr, A. (2003) „Globalisierung der Weltwirtschaft", Band 24, Bremen.
5. Schmidt, P. (2001), "German American Chamber of Commerce – New York", in Trade Magazine, June 2001
6. Schmidt, P. (2002a), "Die amerikanische und die deutsche Wirtschaftskultur im Vergleich", 4. Auflage, Göttingen.
7. Schmidt, P. (2002b), "American and German Communication Styles – Bridging Cultural Differences", speech at the M&A Symposium in Ingolstadt
8. Schmidt, P. (2003a), „American openness…or is it just superficiality with a smile?"
9. Schmidt, P. (2003b), "'American` openness…German ´objectivity`"', speech at the Goethe Institute in Chicago, September 2003.
10. Schmidt, P. (2004), "Non-Conventional Truths about American-German Business", in Trade Magazine, April 2004.
11. Stewart, E.; Milton, J. B. (1991), „American cultural patterns", Intercultural Press, Maine.
12. www.agcc.de
13. www.amcham.com
14. www.german-connection.com
15. www.umanitoba.ca